from the library of

 B Is For

Bad Poetry

B Is For

Bad Poetry

PAMELA AUGUST RUSSELL

STERLING

New York / London
www.sterlingpublishing.com

STERLING and the distinctive Sterling logo are registered trademarks of
Sterling Publishing Co., Inc.

Library of Congress Cataloging-in-Publication Data Available

10 9 8 7 6 5 4 3 2 1

Published by Sterling Publishing Co., Inc.
387 Park Avenue South, New York, NY 10016
© 2009 by Pamela August Russell
Distributed in Canada by Sterling Publishing
c/o Canadian Manda Group, 165 Dufferin Street
Toronto, Ontario, Canada M6K 3H6
Distributed in the United Kingdom by GMC Distribution Services
Castle Place, 166 High Street, Lewes, East Sussex, England BN7 1XU
Distributed in Australia by Capricorn Link (Australia) Pty. Ltd.
P.O. Box 704, Windsor, NSW 2756, Australia

Designed by Brian MacMullen

Printed in the United States of America
All rights reserved

Sterling ISBN 978-1-4027-6787-6

For information about custom editions, special sales, premium and
corporate purchases, please contact Sterling Special Sales
Department at 800-805-5489 or specialsales@sterlingpublishing.com.

For
Bud and Alice Travers

CONTENTS

This Just In

Sources confirm
the woman who
stole your heart
has been arrested.
Police in Reno say
she was disguised
as a beautiful soul
who would never
hurt a fly.
Detectives also say
she is wanted
in several other states
for impersonating
someone who actually
gave a shit about you.

The State Of California vs. Ex-Lover #17

Your Honor, I had to
cut off her legs
to make sure she wouldn't
come waltzing back into my life.

Nietzsche And The Ice-Cream Truck

God is dead.
But this atomic
berry blast Popsicle
is heavenly.

Notes On My First Day Of Therapy

My mother
a knife
a getaway car.

A Beginner's Guide To Mediocrity

Try not to dream.
It's futile and you might as well
wish for the end of gravity.

Be part of the herd.
No one likes an original voice
especially if it's louder than theirs.

Learn to live with irony and regret.
Everyone knows
it's all we have left.

Get used to your mortality.
It will eventually consume you
so why not pick up an addiction.

Don't bother getting out of bed.
The world is crowded enough
without you and your big ideas.

Betty Crocker's Oven-Free Cookbook Tops The Bestseller List In Hell

"Look," said Hitler to Hess,
"I made Himmler a cake
for his birthday." "Mmm,
so moist and fluffy," said Hess,
"and it practically baked itself!"

Tea For Two (A Tragedy)

For Richard Brautigan, who couldn't be with us

It wasn't until after
I poured the second cup
that I realized
I was alone.

Subterranean Abstraction

In Hell,
just before lunch
Gandhi is waving
a gun around
demanding a steak.

How To Reprimand A Cynical Optimist

You can have your cake
and eat it too
but don't let me catch you
five minutes later
in the bathroom
with your finger
down your throat.

Friggin' Houdini

You disappear
right before my eyes
through a trap door
in your soul.
Three weeks later
while I'm folding laundry
you reappear
in a haze of smoke
holding the queen of hearts
and ask, 'Is this your card?'

But L'ORÉAL Said I Was Worth It

I still look ridiculous
no matter how much
expensive makeup
I put on every time you
walk out the door.

Motto

When one door closes
another door opens
onto a cliff.

A Brief History Of Feminism

Sally sells seashells
by the seashore
as if people didn't know
you could just
go to the beach
and find them yourself.

Schadenfreude Encore

I watched you fall
in love again
and couldn't help
but laugh.

Cubist Questionnaire

    If Picasso can turn
    his lover into a starfish
    I'm sure I can turn you
    into _____?

The Girl Finally Gets It

Don't come any closer or I'll scream
halt or I'll shoot
everybody stay where you are
stand back she could blow
yes that's him, officer
keep walking nothing to see here
nobody move or the girl gets it
right on the lips, pal.

The Definition Of Beauty Sandwich

What you see
is what you get
what you see?

The Forgotten Art Of Mincing Words

Oh good, you're back.
Did you get the sausage
like I asked?
The spicy, Polish kielbasa?
You forgot it?
How could you?
All I wanted was
some damn sausage
and I don't think I'm
asking much here!
I even gave you a note
it said, "don't forget the sausage,"
and you forgot the sausage!
This is so typical of you.
This is unforgivable.
This is . . .
what I'm trying to say is,
I'm in love with you.

Epitaph On A Hair

Here lies, at the end of the drain
A gray lock of hair dyed red
I'll never quite know of its pain
While tearing it from my head.

Now it clings to the tub for life
Dancing a watery jig
Never again to be combed or styled
Unless it ends up in a wig.

Fellini Teaches Community College

Forget about writer's block.
If it's any consolation,
even the typewriter is depressed.

Despair, Party Of One

Despair, party of one
your table is ready
I'm sorry, my mistake
actually it's not
it'll probably be
another forty-five minutes
maybe more . . .
Sorry.

So Much For *The Tibetan Book Of The Dead*

If life hands you a noose
don't fret or whine
they'll still cook your goose
in a matter of time
the Earth won't stand still
the Sun won't implode
just sign the damn will
while they lock and load
when the hairdryer's ready
to drop in the bath
with their hands nice and steady
well, you do the math
keep your fingers crossed
and with any luck
by the time you're gone
you won't give a fuck.

Capitalism Can Fall Not Like I Fell For You

I should sell my broken heart
on the open market
in Europe or Asia
fill up my empty cavity
with gold bars, diamonds and yen
maybe then you'd take stock
of how much we lost.

You're Like Dolly Parton Only You're Not

You're like Dolly Parton
only you're not
in love with me
the way she loves
a hot pink electric guitar.

Autobiography

Looks like a pump,
feels like a sneaker.
Looks like a pump,
feels like a sneaker.

The Decline Of Postmodern Civilization

Of all the watches melting on branches
Of all the splattered canvases in Montauk
Of all the soup cans that came before you
Of all these fragments I have shored
against these ruins. Of all the errant knights
in search of chivalry, David Foster Wallace
doesn't want to be here anymore.

Fictional Photo Shoot Conversation

Photographer: "The girl in the burlap dress looks uncomfortable."

Assistant: "Probably because no one is talking to her."

Mata Hari

No one will ever know
you were the worst kisser
in the world.
Even if they put a gun
to my head and force me
to say it in a poem.

All These Years And You're Still Saddled With Intimacy Issues

"It's not the *vagina dentata*
I'm worried about," he said.
"It's just that you haven't
been brushing and flossing."

Now She's In Movies

Once she faked an orgasm
and didn't tell me
for three years.
She calls me from L.A.
to say now she's in movies.

Crazy Things Happen If You Fall Asleep Listening To The Beatles

Paul is dead
and I'm pretty
darn sure
I am the eggman.

College Notebook

Existentialism can be applied to anything.
Every moment is a continuous choice.
How do we find meaning?
Kegger at Bryce Hall 3:30 P.M.

Thanks For The Ether

I tried to leave L.A.
only to get stuck
in traffic.
Now what?

Ode To A Summer Vacation

Our small island
off the coast of Maine
was like a weekend in bed
with champagne and old movies.
Coming home to L.A.
is like a bathroom full of junkies
cleaning blood off the walls
arguing about where to get more.

Polaroid

That's a nice sunset
in the background
but you look sad.

Zebra

It's too bad you think
life is so black and white.
If you had four legs and a tail
we could at least talk.

Joni Mitchell Configuration

Oh, I could drink
a case of you
and then pass out
in my own vomit.
When the EMTs arrive
to pump my stomach,
I'll still be slurring
your name.
Oh, I'll still be slurring
your name.

Bury My Heart At Wounded Knee

Bury my heart
at wounded knee
or sprained ankle
even torn ligament,
but please don't
bury it alone.

Not All Literature Is Gossip

To hell with Capote.
You should read Baldwin.
Now *there's* a genius.

The New Testament Delicatessen

From the book of Matthew
(Chapter One: Verse eighteen)
1:18
"These are the facts
concerning the birth
of Jesus Christ.
"His mother Mary
was to be engaged
to marry Joseph
but
while she was still a virgin
she became pregnant
by the holy spirit."*

*Ham, turkey, roast beef
on rye. Hold the meat.*

Dorothy Parker Laments

If I said, "You're right, it's true."
You'd only half believe me.
If I said, "It's done, we're through."
You'd say, "Then leave the key."
If I said, "No point in talking,
it's only useless chatter."
With a nod and a wink
you'd pour me a drink and ask,
"Ah, but did we matter?"

Love Is Like A Toilet Bowl

Love is like
a toilet bowl.
One touch
and you too
could be in
deep shit.

Unfortunate Cookie

You will soon meet someone
who will bring you much joy and love.

Eventually they will devour your soul
like it's a hot dog eating championship.

Lucky Numbers: 543, 8, 192, 78

How To Save A Tangerine From Suffering

Never peel it.
Use it to practice
juggling instead.
Give it a name.

We Could Have Danced All Night

We could have danced all night,
except
your
eyes
      are
like
empty
ballrooms.

Everybody Loves You At 3:00 A.M.

For Kathlyn Horan with apologies to Zelda Fitzgerald

It was
so sad
to see
you go
off in
your new
rhumba
panties
alone.

Recipe For Disaster

1 teaspoon vanilla extract
$1^2/_3$ cup sugar
3 eggs
I love him
$^3/_4$ cup butter or margarine (softened)
but I'm not 'in love' with him
$^1/_2$ cup cream (unsweetened)
1 cup all-purpose flour
we're getting married
$^2/_3$ cup cocoa
tomorrow
$^1/_4$ cup baking powder

(beat until blended)

She Wants Chocolate

She wants chocolate
and I have
the knife wounds
to prove it.

The Cheese Poem

"Poets have been mysteriously silent on the subject of cheese."
—G. K. CHESTERTON

Gouda, Brie, Fontina,
Feta, Parmesan, Cow's Milk,
Limburger, Roquefort, Havarti,
Blue, Romano, Cottage.
There. I've milked it
for all it's worth.

Despite The Calamities

You could have said yes
but you didn't
I could have said no
but I wouldn't
you could have been mine
but you shouldn't
since I can be unkind
but I won't.

The Dean Martin Defense

When the moon hits your eye
like a big pizza pie
just say you ran into a door.

Popeye, Hamlet & Sartre
(A Rendering)

I am what I am
today, anyway
which is to say
this is not
what I was
yesterday, or that
I'm even thinking
about tomorrow,
so for the most part,
you're looking at it.
Sort of.

Sadness You Old Minx

I even have trouble
parallel parking
on a lonely road.

Flimflammer

I've been working you over
like a Thai masseuse.
I'm a greasy bard,
a shardy demoiselle,
a huckster in training
perfecting the short con
for a longer kiss with you.

Riding Bitch With Rosemary Clooney
& Peggy Lee

You with the stars
in your eyes
put them back
in the sky.
You're ruining it
for the rest of us.

Meet Me In Tiananmen Square

You're like a tank
rolling into my heart,
unwelcomed.
When I ask,
"Why are you here?
You've caused nothing
but misery."
I am never seen
or heard from again.

Mauvais Rêve

(In Memoriam, New Orleans, August 2005)

I had a dream.
In it, Rosa Parks nods
politely to the driver
takes her seat quietly
in the back of the bus
and begins to sew
furiously.

Miserable'

Miserable'
Miserable'
Toute le journe
je suis miserable'
mon Coeur
reste sur une étagère
je reste sur une etegere
nettoye l'etagere
sale étagère.
C'est toi, c'est tois!
C'est toi que j'aime
et pourtant je suis miserable'
et puis je fume.
Je suis miserable'.

Miserable

Miserable,
Miserable.
All day long
I am miserable.
My heart
it sits on a shelf
I sit on a shelf
clean the shelf
dirty shelf!
It is you, it is you!
It is you that I love
and yet I am miserable
and so I smoke.
I am miserable.

Film Noir Haiku

I'm rich and you cheat.
With me dead the money's yours.
Soon my brakes will fail.

Torture Haiku

Alright already
Alright already, darling
Alright already

Chocolate & Flour Union—Local 133
(Meeting Notes)

It has come to our attention that
the cupcakes have organized and decided
you folks are lookin' a little chubby.

Platitude Omelet

I've been walking
on eggshells ever since
I heard you say,
'She seems nice.'

I Became A Fabulous Opera

It is recovered! What? Eternity. It is the sea mixed with the sun.
—RIMBAUD

I became
a fabulous opera
the day the fat lady
began to sing
completely out of tune.

Security Question
(Please Choose One)

A) What is your mother's maiden name?

B) What is the name of your first pet?

C) What is it with your heart that it breaks so easy?

The New Dawn

I awaken
the first day
in my new apartment
to the sound
of the neighbor's
reaching orgasm
in a frenzy of
"Ungh-ungh-ungh's."
It's enough to make
a single gal reach
for a high-fat snack.

Kiss Me Quick

Kiss me quick
before I have
that dream again.
The one where I'm
riding a zebra naked
through Chelsea
during rush hour
and you go whizzing by
on a shiny silver scooter
yelling something like,
"I love you!"
but I can't be sure
because of the police sirens
so I yell back,
"I love you, too!"
When a nun carrying
a huge red bong
comes up and says,
"She didn't say '*I love you.*'
She said '*You have toilet paper
stuck to your shoe.*'"

The Perfect Love Poem

Every time
I see your face
it reminds me
of you.

A Lady Writing

She must have sat for weeks
with that pen in her hand
thinking of all the things
she'd like to say
if she could move
while Vermeer took his
sweet time painting her.

B Is For Bad Poetry

For Lise Bargardo

Bad poetry!
You can just
sit in the corner
until you learn
how to rhyme.

Inappropriately Touched By An Angel

Once upon a time
there was an imaginary woman
who was very pleased
whenever she met a genius
or anyone who could juggle
kitchen knives or fruit.
"Well," she'd say,
"you'll have to pass the equator again,
your feet should dissolve
where the soles fail to settle."
"Oh, and you should never smell
like Chanel No. 5 or Dior
but of glue and paint, and yes,
your nails should be dirty."
"Isn't she wonderful?" I'd ask.
"No," They'd say. "She's a drunk
and a whore who's always humming
or yelling obscenities in Portuguese."
I can hear that funny little tune
and I'm drawn like a magnet to that place.

When in an uncertain whirl of smoke
she demanded that:
I not feel small among gifted women &
A Harvey Wallbanger
After a few, she began to babble.
"I'm sorry," she said,
"for acting like art is such a bitch.
Could it be the same with love?"
Years later, while clipping my toenails,
I discovered I was the mirror of the universe.
"Finally!" She screamed. "You should get out
and create a few scars, kiss a few lips,
you know, go on living. And never count a woman out
until she swallows huge amounts of aspirin."
Anyway, I knew someday she'd be back
embracing the planets, wearing tighter clothes
and yelling at me to never be famous
for what I really am, lazy.

The Janis Joplin Of It All

We tried.
We even tried
just a little bit harder.
It's not working.

Higgledy-Piggledy

Higgledy-piggledy
Helen of Troy
Heckuva gal
Helluva decoy

Speaking of wooden horses
A ruse and a con
Been screwing someone else
Saddle up, moving on!

The Trouble With Starfish

Last night I dreamt
all the starfish
in the ocean
were mad at me.
To prove it they
sucked the seas dry
leaving them empty.
I woke up
with a terrible hangover.

The Trouble With Comedians

Last night I dreamt
I was in a room full of comics
who were confused because
bubbles were coming
out of their mouths
when they talked.
I told them it's because
they're under water.
To thank me for
pointing this out,
they made me their
favorite joke writer.
I woke up
feeling kind of funny.

The Trouble With Birthday Cakes

Last night I dreamt
I had the chicken pox
at my birthday party.
I blew out the candles
and made a wish
but no one wanted cake
because they thought
I got germs all over it.
I woke up
and remembered I was single.

The Prayers Of An Insomniac

Betelgeuse consume me
sparkle for the blind man in the alley
pissing away hope
Oh, mother of cirrhosis
make me a drink.
Put me in a cement party frock
make me tango all alone
or waltz me into the gutter
Oh, fear of destiny
seduce me.
Wet my whistle & when the train comes
put a dime on the track to stop me
Oh, transporter of desire
quench mine.
Big night sky,
tear off my dress
kiss my swollen lips
Oh, lover of mortality
let me catch my breath.
Bivouac of thieves
climb with me up to the Milky Way
help me pry the stars out of the sky
Oh, sweet mystery of darkness
Let me rest!

Tarantella

An ice cube
in an empty glass
more gin
more sway
in the hips
less fear and melancholy
after we danced
for thirty-five minutes
after we kissed
like fifth graders
after I threw up
on your coat
and after you left
without your socks
I thought to myself
too bad,
we could have
really had something.

Urbane Decay

There are weeds now
where your tongue
once circled
broken beer bottles
and rusted car parts
where your hands
once caressed
graffiti and paint chips
where your lips
once kissed
and a tow truck
taking away
the only orgasm left
on this empty lot

More Fun At The Gertrude Stein
Home For Wayward Girls

Here is a sentence.
It makes no sense yet
I was asked to leave
by Gertrude, bye
when Alice and I
Oh, look. A statement.
Kissed. A verb.
I blame
the pot brownies
Alice made and she
made out with me
and Alice
are trouble in
that
we're in it.

Elephant

There's an elephant
in the room.
He's wearing your
favorite T-shirt,
cooked us a delightful
lasagna for dinner
and left a note
on the fridge that says,
"You should break up."
I wonder what he wants?

Effigy And Excuse

It's not you, it's me.
Or someone like me
only much worse.

Normally I Wouldn't

Normally I wouldn't
ask if you love me
but when I saw
all my things
on the lawn
I got curious.

So It Is Not With Me As With That Damn Muse

She comes
and goes
like an amateur
hooker.
Leaving me alone
with my
imagination.

Somewhere The Dog Got Off The Boat

Somewhere the dog
of us got off the boat
and is lost at sea.
I keep thinking
I'm swimming toward you,
I keep thinking
the tide will pull us in,
I keep thinking I see
a helicopter in the distance
but it's just a seagull.

The Plight

Virginia Woolf put stones in her pocket
and wandered off into the sea.
My mother always said
I have rocks in my head
I wonder what will become of me?

If I Had A Gun

.

Napoléon In Vain

No matter how many times
I try to conquer
my fear of intimacy
I always come up short.

Showdown At The *I'm Not O.K. Yet* Corral

This town ain't big enough
for the both of us since
I keep running into you
and your new girlfriend
at restaurants and bookstores.
Shall we say pistols at dawn?

Some Not-So-Enchanted Evening

I had the homemade meatloaf
you thought you saw a woman
who looked a lot like your wife.
We talked about buying a Bowflex®
home gym together but in between
the spinach dip you said it felt
like too much of a commitment.
After dessert I was full
of resentment. On top of that,
you remind me of my father.

Donner Party Review

I tried to take
a shortcut
to your heart
instead I got lost
in the wilderness
of my own desire.

Metaphor Diarrhea

I'm falling in love with you
like the rain full of intent
like a bear in a garbage can
like an engine leaking oil
like a robber in your jewelry drawer
like a doctor with a knife
like a new electric razor
like autumn in Central Park,
I'm changing.

Give Me Elaine Stritch Or Give Me Death

If she goes—
there ain't no more
dames left on Broadway
to drink & smoke with
tell us we're full of shit,
off key and not worth
the gum/stuck to the bottom
of our tap shoes.
Still we listen
to the song
of that siren
'til she transforms us
into beasts.

Sandy Dennis Briefly

I wake up
to my cats
judging me.
They stare
blankly
as if to say,
"Is this what
you had in mind
for your life?
If it is, you may
want to consider
sleeping pills or
a tall bridge
because in our view,
you're pathetic."

Or

they're hungry.

The World Is Going To Hell In A Handbag

And I waited gluttonously
for Christ or some savior
other than cheap wine and chocolate.
Turns out, he's in a restroom
off highway five pulling splinters out of his hand so he can
masturbate
before his cheeseburger arrives.

Birds I View

They teeter on telephone wires
nervous and aware they
stare, coo and they're gone.
Like all of my ex-lovers.

Following Khrushchev

I've been following Khrushchev
through the snow
on our way to lunch
near the Kremlin.
He's walking very fast
and all I can think is
where are we really going?

Illumination Handyman

The light at the end of the tunnel
needs to be replaced.

How I Made Sense Of You

Trying to make
sense of you
was like flogging
a dead horse,
with a dead horse.

Sing-A-Long With The Cocteau Twins

She'll go hiccup and drown
Should I hiccup?
Makes her eggs stop and tongue go
Should I hiccup?
And it's catchy and brown
Should I hiccup?
Makes her hips sore at school
Should I hiccup?
Should I hiccup?
I'm curious.

Country Song Poem

There's a lonesome teardrop hangin'
from the corner of your eye
better pull down that ol' cowboy hat
so the moon don't see you cry.

Somewhere east of Amarillo
a woman who hasn't slept
for years bought a pillow.

(Guitar Solo)

There but for the grace go I
scraping my fingers against the sky
plucking out a star or two
one for me, a pretty song for you.

A Mystery To Me

My ego is bigger than a bread box.
I'm always late and don't seem to mind.
I have seven cavities.
I'm not sure what to say when you're sad.
I forget to shower on a regular basis.
I'm easily disappointed by strangers.
I prefer lying over ignorance.
I hate cauliflower.
I need you.
Who am I?

Rotten In Denmark

Dare I ask about our love anymore?
The question circles above us
like a pack of vultures
and when the time comes,
they'll feed well on the carcass
of uncertainty.

Diamante For A Crappy Relationship

You
Useless, Selfish
Drinking, Burping, Cheating
Ballsy, Gun-toting, Pointing, Laughing
Police-calling, Arresting
Me

Poetic Injustice

If they paid more money
I'd be writing novels.

Relativity Theory For A Melancholy Gal

Some days go by
like elephants.
Other days go by
like elephants
with water retention
and bloating.

Conjugating You

We think you're boring.
You are kind of mean.
Why is she still here?

Paranoid Novella

"Are you okay?" I asked,
not sure what to say.
"Is there anything I can do?"
"No," she said, "I think
you've done quite enough."

We Don't Call Her Einstein For Nothing

So what if she's
going nowhere
at the speed of light.
She'll still end up here
in front of this mirror
where she figures if she
stares long enough, eventually
she can seduce herself.

Excuses

Would the owner
of the red Ford
pick-up truck
please move it.
You're blocking
the writer's mind.

Hallmark Nightmare

Dear blank,

Thinking of you
while you are gone
as I lay here
beside you,
I feel so alone.

As always,
Blank

Hindsight

I can tell you now
when you sat naked
on the edge of my lips
and whispered
how good it all felt,
maybe I shouldn't
have told you
to shut up.

Plate Tectonics And Us

When two oceanic plates meet each other
(oceanic–oceanic) this often results
in the formation of an island arc system.
As the subducting oceanic crust melts
as it goes deeper into the Earth,
the newly-created magma rises
to the surface and forms volcanoes.
If the activity continues, the volcano
may grow tall enough to breech the surface
of the ocean creating an island.
So make the bed and put the coffee on.
It's your turn.

It's Not Because I'm Dirty

It's not because
I'm clean,
it's not because
I kissed a girl
behind a magazine.
It's because at breakfast,
when you asked me
if I loved you,
I was all caught
up in an article
about Brad & Angie
and when I looked up
you were gone.

Jump Rope Reality Show

B my name is Barbara
my husband's name is Ben
we're from Boston
and we're bisexual.
At least I am.
I think Ben's just
going along with it
because he's afraid
of losing me since I met

L her name is Lucy
her girlfriend's name is Liz
they're both lesbians
but I'm not sure
what to do
because I still love Ben
Oh, I'm so confused.

Can we turn off
the cameras, please?

The World Is Not A Safe Place

The world is not a safe place for lovers.
For instance, mine was hit by a bus.

Letters To A Young Poet

I would stick with R and M
and your choice of a decent vowel
preferably A.

Dear Poet,
Do it for the money. Spend it all on booze and tweed coats until
you end up at McLean Hospital with electrodes attached to your head.
Keep writing anyway on dirty floors, walls and mattresses 'til they
pry the empty pen from your warm, capable hand.

Lizzie Borden Has The Last Word

Nobody's immortal.
But some of us live
to write about it.